Picking Up the Pieces After Divorce: Working Through the Healing Process

By Andrea M. Stuckey

Table of Contents

Introduction

As you are feeling the pain that you're going through during the process of divorce recovery, you may wonder what the future holds for you and your family. When you find yourself at the end of your marriage and going through the litigation process, oftentimes, the pain is unbearable. The pain of divorce is greater than dealing with death. When the covenant has been broken and the vow that you have set before God and your family and friends literally tears your heart apart. Oftentimes, there is no one word that can explain the feeling of what it's like to go through the process of divorce. Even though you are going through this process it is very important that you feel the pain and identify all the emotions that you're feeling.

The divorce recovery process is just that it is a process. Your emotions will have you feeling like you're on a roller coaster. One day you will be up feeling excited about your new life, and on another day, you will be close to the state of depression. It is important to recognize that these feelings of highs and lows is very normal as you're going through a separation or divorce. I speak of the separation process because oftentimes, you may have left the marriage, are physically living apart, but the final divorce piece of that puzzle has not taken place yet. It can sometimes take years, and unfortunately you are living as though you are single and already divorced. It's just that the legal documentation has not taken place. The real reasons that ended the marriage aren't relevant because there is still a general emotional process that you must experience through after a marriage has ended. Some of the things that spur a divorce may be infidelity, financial issues, communication issues, addictions, various forms of abuse, domestic, emotional, and financial abuse as well. There is an array of reasons that people find themselves in the divorce court. What I have found after being divorced twice, is that what the actual reason for the divorce does not matter, the process of recovery remains the same.

There are 6 stages in the process of divorce recovery. In this book, we will focus on important actions that will help you pick up the pieces and move forward with your life.

There are also a couple of emotions that are not a stage of the divorce recovery process, but many people who go through a divorce, feel that these certain feelings are holding them back from moving forward with their lives. Rejection, guilt, shame, low self-esteem, and the inability to make decisions can often keep you feeling stuck.

Over 50% of marriages end in divorce and oftentimes the possible long lasting effects are minimized in today's society. Learn how to pick up those pieces of your life, and put them back together, so that you can frame your life in any way that you desire.

The Stages of Grief During Divorce

Elizabeth Kubler-Ross has written profound information about the various stages of grief following loss. Divorce is a loss and causes deep emotional pain and grief. Someone who is grieving may go through the following stages in any order, during the divorce process.

Denial- "This can't really be happening"

There is refusal to accept the fact that the separation or divorce has occurred. Oftentimes the situation is minimalized or blatantly denied. It is important to accept what is happening to prevent prolonging the stage of denial.

Pain and Fear - "What am I going to do?" "How will I be able to move forward?"

In this stage there is real emotional pain and fear of what the future is going to look like in many different areas of life. This stage is paralyzing and can prevent action of physical activities that must be taken care of.

Anger – "Why is this happening to me?"

During this stage, there is often blaming of oneself and others. There may be reoccurring arguments between you and your spouse about varying issues that are occurring during the divorce process.

Bargaining – *"I will do anything to change this situation."*

In this stage, the individual tries to delay the divorce or may try to convince themselves that the marriage can be worked out. They may also try to convince their spouse to return to the marriage.

Depression – *"What's the point of going on anyway?"*

During depression, the fact that the divorce is real and going to happen is recognized. Oftentimes, an individual may isolate themselves from others, spend time grieving and crying. Depression truly has a clear view of what has taken place, though hurtful.

Acceptance – *"It's going to be alright."*

Finally, the divorce is accepted and understood logically and emotionally. This is goal of the divorce recovery process.

Can you recognize which divorce recovery stage that you are currently in?

____
____
____
____
____

____

What are some ways that you can identify with that stage?

____

____

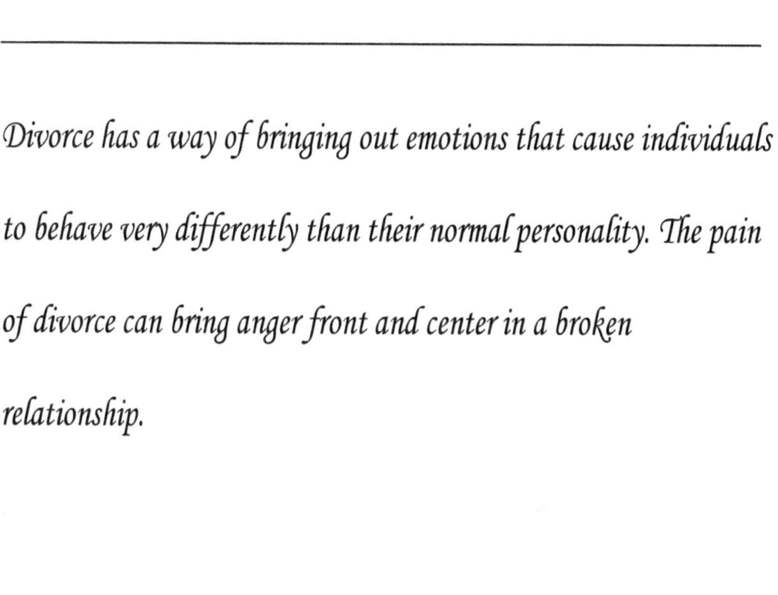

Divorce has a way of bringing out emotions that cause individuals to behave very differently than their normal personality. The pain of divorce can bring anger front and center in a broken relationship.

Overcoming Anger

Anger is not good or bad, it is an emotion. It is important to feel your emotions and try to identify what is causing them, so that you can put it in perspective, and begin to release it. You may feel angry because your mate did or said something specifically hurtful or you may just be angry because the relationship has broken down. Whatever the reason, the anger in a divorce can be extreme and vindictive. It is an anger that has usually never been experienced before. If not controlled, anger can become a destructive force in your life.

Writing your feelings down is a great way to release them, without hurting someone else.

Andrea M. Stuckey ©2016

1. List the top 3 three things that you are angry about.

    a. ___________________________________

    b. ___________________________________

    c. ___________________________________

2. Write a letter to your spouse expressing all the reasons why you are feeling angry.

____

____

____

____

____

____

____

____

____

____

____

____

____

You can keep the letter, or you can throw it away. Write as many letters as you need to, to release your anger.

When picking up the pieces of your life following divorce, there are some actions that must be done to begin to move forward with the next chapter of your life.

The Revelation of Reflection

Reflection on your past marriage is vital. Even though the thoughts may be painful, it is very necessary to reflect. Reflecting allows you to recognize the real issues that took place in the marriage. This is not about blame ; it is first about facts.

Everyone has played a part in the breakdown in the relationship in some way, shape, or form.

For example, there may have been problems in any of the following areas: finances, communication, sex, work, stress, children(discipline), living arrangements, emotional abuse, physical abuse, co-dependency, control issues, jealousy, insecurity, attraction, personal boundaries, blended families, social disagreements, or health issues.

Andrea M. Stuckey ©2016

Identify 3 main areas that you know were difficult in your marriage.

1. _______________________________________
2. _______________________________________
3. _______________________________________

1. *What was the specific problem in each area? (Example: Work- both spouses worked too much, therefore not able to spend quality one on one time.)*
   a. _______________________________________
      ____
   b. _______________________________________
      ____
   c. _______________________________________
      ____

2. *How did you contribute to each problem? Be honest. Own your art. (Example: When we had an opportunity to spend time together, I chose to work instead.)*

____

____

____

____

____

____

____

3. *In hindsight, in each area, what could you have done differently? Think and be specific. (Example: I could have prioritized and planned for the need of our one on one time together.)*

____

____

____

____

____

____

Those exercises allow you to own your part of the breakdown of the relationship. They reveal areas where you could have made a difference. Once you admit and own that, you can move forward, and commit to working on one area of your life for yourself. If you don't work on you, whenever you chose to date or enter another relationship, you will have the same behavior and traits, and thus you will attract the same type of person that you are. Believe it or not, we attract what we are, not what we want.

"Broken attracts broken."

Finding Freedom in Forgiveness

Divorce brings out a rollercoaster of emotions as previously discussed. Emotions of anger, bitterness, guilt and shame can stay in your life, hinder your spiritual, emotional, and social growth.

The Bible talks about the root of bitterness growing in your heart in Hebrews 12:15. When these emotions are not released, they grow deeper into our heart, the harder they are to release.

Forgiveness is a very important part of your healing process. It's tough to accept, but regardless of what someone has done, you need to forgive them. Forgiving someone does not mean that you agree with what has happened, nor are you saying that it is okay. You are forgiving them, just as God has forgiven you. Forgiveness allows you to release and let go, so that you can be free. You may *never get an apology or a person may never even ask for your forgiveness, but you can forgive them anyway. When you don't forgive, essentially you are allowing another person to have power over you. Oftentimes, they have gone on with their lives, and you are still angry about what they have done, and you are remaining immobilized in your life. In addition, oftentimes, shame or guilt may weigh you down as well. Just as you forgive others, you also need to forgive yourself.*

"If you forgive other people when they sin against you, your heavenly Father will also forgive you." Matthew 6:14

What 3 areas are you holding on to? Who or what do you need to release.?

1. _______________________________
2. _______________________________
3. _______________________________

Take time to write out what it is that you want to forgive, release and let go of. Write down what has happened, and how it has made you feel. Getting your emotions out of your head is often a great way to begin to release and let go.

____

____

____

____

Moving Forward in the Next Chapter of Your Life

You have reflected, and released, and now you can begin to move forward in your life. Divorce is a very traumatic experience, however choose to take a negative experience for what it is, and turn it into a positive. Positive in the aspect that you have an opportunity to change the course of your life if you choose. You can repave the path of your life if you choose to put in the work for YOU!

What are 3 things that you know that are your talents, strengths, or that you are simply good at? List them. Are you using those talents? How or why not?

1. ____

   ____

2. ____

   ____

3. ____

   ____

Recognizing your gifts are important. God created us very uniquely, and we should be using our gifts in some way, shape or form. Operating in those gifts, brings us joy and happiness. Oftentimes, we allow the opinions and views of others to steer us away from those gifts. It is time to be true to yourself. Identify those gifts, and use them even if they are on a hobby level, or a business or occupational level. Evaluate how you can use your

gifts in this next chapter of your life.

In addition to your gifts, begin to look at the following areas of

your life, and identify how you can improve in that area.

List at least one way in each are that you can improve yourself in

some way.

1. Spiritual_______________________________________

____

____

2. Emotional______________________________________

____

____

3. Physical____

____

____

4. Social____

____

____

Picking up the pieces of your life after divorce is a process. It takes time. You deserve to give yourself this time. Be patient with yourself, and give yourself the grace you need, and the time that you need to fully heal.

Divorce does not disqualify you from all that life has to offer. No matter what your age, there is so much more life to live. You will be able to fully live again, intently laugh again, and if you desire, love again.

Gather the courage to pick up the pieces of the puzzle of your life, one by one. Take your time as you figure out where all the pieces go. Put them together at your pace, and in the end, you'll have a beautiful finished product to frame and cherish forever.

Andrea M. Stuckey ©2016

Andrea M. Stuckey Bio

Andrea M. Stuckey is passionate about helping women through the devastating life changes that come along with separation and divorce. She is the Founder of Live Life Luvd LLC, where she is dedicated to helping women rebuild their lives through transformational life coaching, speaking and writing. She is the author of <u>Suddenly Single: A Woman's Spiritual and Practical Guide to the First 5 Years Following Separation and Divorce</u> which can be purchased on <u>www.amazon.com</u>. She teaches women how to cultivate and activate their gifts and talents, to redefine their lives and pursue their dreams. Having gone through divorce twice, she empowers women, shares her journey, and gives spiritual and practical tips that are applicable to live a liberated lifestyle.

Andrea is available for speaking engagements and workshops for divorce support groups, and women empowerment meetings and conferences.

Stay connected with her on the following platforms:

andrea@livelifeluvd.com

www.livelifeluvd.com

www.twitter.com/livelifeluvd

www.instagram.com/livelifeluvd

www.facebook.com/livlifeluvd

www.periscope.tv/livelifeluvd

Private Facebook group   bit.ly/divorceeliberation

Dear Divorcee Blog   bit.ly/deardivorcee

9 781543 096101